# God Loves You

TEXT/ Carol Rubow

EDITOR/ Walter M. Wangerin

ART/ Concordia Films

Concordia Publishing House, St. Louis, Missouri
Concordia Publishing House Ltd., London, E. C. 1
© 1968 by Concordia Publishing House
MANUFACTURED IN THE UNITED STATES OF AMERICA

Concordia Publishing House
St. Louis          London

Many, many people live in the world.

Some are tall people
and some are short people.

Some are thin people
and some are fat people.

Some are young people
and some are old people.

Many, many people
live in the world.

Some of these people love you very much.

Mother loves you.
Father loves you.
Grandmother loves you.
Grandfather loves you.

Many people love you very much.

Do you know who else loves you very much?

God loves you.        God loves Mother.        God loves Grandmother.

                      God loves Father.        God loves Grandfather.

God loves YOU very much.

Did you know that God made you?
God made everything in the world.

God made the bright, pretty flowers.
God made the tall, tall trees.

God made animals that run.     God made birds that fly.
God made animals that hop.     God made fish that swim.

God made you.
God made everything in the world.

Did you know that once
there was no world?


There were no
bright, pretty flowers.
There were no
tall, tall trees.
There were no
animals that run or hop.
There were no
birds that fly.
There were no
fish that swim.

There was only God. . . .

God said,
    "Let there be flowers!"
And there were flowers.

God said,
    "Let there be trees!"
And there were trees.

God said,

"Let there be animals!"
And there were animals.

God made everything in the world

12

Can you make a bright, pretty flower?
Can you make a tall, tall tree?
Can you make a real, live rabbit?
NO! NOBODY CAN!
There are some things only God can do.

Only God can make the rain fall.
Only God can make the sun shine.
Only God can make the wind blow.
Only God can make the flowers grow.
There is something else
only God can do . . .

Only God can see you
   ALL the time.

God sees you
   when you sleep at night.
God sees you
   when you play outside.
God sees you
   when you read in school.
God sees you
   when you pray in church.

God sees you
   ALL the time.

God loves you.
God sees you
    and keeps you safe.
Are you ever afraid?

Are you
afraid
at night
when
it is very,
very dark?

Are you afraid
when you hear
a loud, loud noise?

You do not need to be afraid.
God knows where you are.
God takes care of you all the time.
God gave you Mother and Father to tak
care of you.
God sends His holy angels to watch ove
you and keep you safe.

18

Why does God
   love people so much?
Why does God
   give people so many things?

Why does God
   take care of people?

That is the way God is.
God is love.
God loves ALL THE TIME!
As God's child
    you want to love too.
But do you love ALL THE TIME?

NO?
Sometimes it's hard to love, isn't it?
Sometimes we do things that hurt people.
Sometimes we say things that hurt people.

Sometimes we think things that hurt people.
Your sin makes you do these things.

Sin is doing what *you* want to do,
not what God wants you to do.
ALL people are sinners.

BUT . . .

When you feel bad
  about this, remember:

God still loves you,
  even when you sin.
God forgives your sin.
God loves you so much . . .

He sent His Son Jesus to save all sinners!
Jesus died on the cross for your sin.

Jesus shows how God loves all people.
Jesus shows how God loves you
even though you sin.

You are God's own dear child.
You can be sure that God forgives your sin.
You can be sure that God loves you.
You can be sure that God will help you love
    Him and all people.

God sends you a special gift to help you love.

God sends His Holy Spirit to live in your heart.

God's Holy Spirit helps you love God.
God's Holy Spirit helps you love other people.
God's Holy Spirit helps you to do the things He wants.

The Holy Spirit is God doing these things in you.

God made you.
God takes care of you.
God forgives your sin because . . .